DOGMAN
The Monsters Are Real

Scott Carpenter

I0440077

Dedication

To anyone who has witnessed something indescribable, unexplainable, and unbelievable.

To those who have kept the secrets to themselves for fear of ridicule and consternation.

To those who have lived with fear and nightmares after encountering an entity that is not supposed to exist.

To those who have carried the burdens of what they have witnessed and experienced for far too long.

To those who can no longer enjoy the outdoors or a moon drenched night for fear of what is lurking in the shadows.

This time it did not get away, this time I have video and you're not crazy!

To Bobbie Short, you will be missed......

Contents

Introduction

I am an amateur Bigfoot researcher. I started doing Bigfoot research in August of 2009 after I had an encounter while fishing. I established two areas that I researched, one on a large track of public land that is approximately fifteen hundred acres in size. The other is various locations within the Great Smokey Mountains National Park.

I was fortunate to be a part of the history making Bigfoot DNA Study that was headed up by Dr. Melba Ketchum and organized by David Paulides. I was invited to become a member of David's research group North American Bigfoot Search (NABS). I participated in the study doing field work submitting over thirty hair and salvia samples to the study. Eleven samples were determined to be from what is known as a Sasquatch or Bigfoot.

During my Bigfoot field work I encountered something that defies logic and explanation. I was not looking for it nor did I know that such a creature existed before I encountered it. This creature found me I did not find it. This entity was not supposed to exist. It is the subject of legends and modern horror movies. It should not be roaming the woods and fields of Eastern Tennessee.

 What is this entity that crashed into my world and shattered my reality? The creature is known by many names but the most common name is the Dogman. Some may know this mythical creature as a Werewolf. The Native Americans call them Skin Walkers. The creature is known as a Rougarou in the swamps of Louisiana.

Whatever name you choose to call it does not matter. What matters is that it is a real biological entity. I know this because during my Bigfoot research I have encountered these Dogmen three times. On the first and third encounter they were lurking close behind me captured on a video camera specifically designed to watch my "back trail". On the second encounter I made direct eye contact with the creature while also capturing video.

This book will contain accounts of all three encounters. The difference in this book and other books about creatures known as "Cryptids" (Creatures whose existence has been suggested but is not yet recognized by scientific consensus) is that I have video! Yes, that is correct. No, your eyes did not deceive you. I have high definition video of the creature known as the Dogman. It is close up and in your face. It is so close that you can see the nostril move as the creature breathes!

So if you're ready to open your mind, and are willing to accept what your eyes see, then proceed, despite what you think you know, the monsters are real!

Chapter 1 – What is a Dogman?

The creature known as a Dogman is approximately five to seven feet tall weighing between two hundred and four hundred pounds. They have the head that resembles a large dog or a wolf with canine ears and a canine-like snout. Some Dogmen have been reported having snouts that are shorter in appearance and flat on the end. Other reports describe a longer snout that appears more canine.

The Dogman is bipedal, walking or running on their "hind legs." They possess a "human-like" torso and arms. They have "claws" for hands. Witnesses have reported seeing the Dogman holding and eating small game clutched in their front "claws."

Below are two sketches I created based on the video footage I have captured of the Dogman.

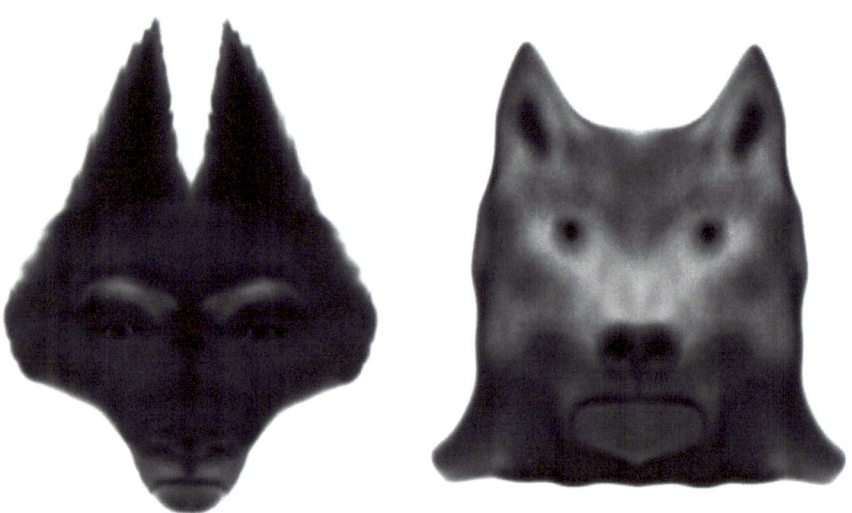

The sketch on the left demonstrates the Dogman that has the longer snout with a canine look. The sketch on the right is the variant that has a shorter snout that is flat on the end. I have encountered both these type creatures.

Dogman Variances

Along with the "traditional" Dogman or Werewolf, there are two other Dogman-like creatures that have been reported.

Bearwolves: Have large bear-like bodies and walk on all fours or upright. They are different from bears in that they have a canine or wolf looking head with a long snout and pointed ears.

Bigfoot Hybrid: Have a Bigfoot-like body with five fingered hands and large human like feet. Wide shoulders, thick muscular chest, and covered with hair over their entire body. The head has a canine or wolf looking appearance with a long snout and pointed canine-like ears. This creature also has been reported by witnesses to have a "mane" of long hair on its head and a "cape" of hair on the shoulders.

Bigfoot Hybrid   "Bearwolf"

Chapter 2 – First Contact

Date: March 27th, 2011

I arrived at my public land Bigfoot research area late morning around 10:30 AM. My plans for the day were to investigate the feeding station and the surrounding area for any sign of Bigfoot activity. A "feeding station" is an area that has been established to leave food for the Bigfoot in the area. I would leave candy bars and apples for the Bigfoot. The Bigfoot in return would bring me "gifts." These gifts included rocks, feathers, and on one occasion a Hawk skull completely bleached and intact.

The feeding station is at the end of a long narrow point of land on a large man-made lake. The area was approximately four acres in size and covered in dense foliage. Off the end of this point was a small island separated from the mainland by an old submerged roadbed. In August of 2009 I had discovered a small clearing on this point that had a shelter made of sticks and vines. I left a gift of five smooth round rocks on a flat piece of broken marble in the shelter. I arranged the rocks in a straight line pattern largest to smallest. I returned the following week to find the rocks had been moved around. The three largest rocks were pushed together at one end of the flat marble with the smallest rock on the other end. The fifth rock had been moved off the flat piece of marble. This formed a 3-1 pattern that would be repeated over and over. This experience convinced me to establish a feeding station in this location.

I investigated the feeding station and found that there had been no activity since my last visit the week before. I began to check the surrounding area for any footprints or sign that the Bigfoot visited the feeding station. I routinely placed black thread between trees that bracket known Bigfoot trails. I put the thread at approximately seven feet off the ground. If a Bigfoot has been walking the trail then it would break the thread. This would alert me to any activity in this area.

I was checking the thread near the feeding station when I captured footage of a Dogman watching me from the cover of thick foliage. The Dogman was behind me and I was not aware of his presence. I had discovered that the Bigfoot are extremely concerned about the direction a researcher is looking. They routinely watched me from behind or followed me. I discovered this by accident when I held my camera pointing behind me while I was putting food out at the feeding station. When I reviewed the footage a Bigfoot had pushed its head through some thick foliage and was watching me from behind. When I stood up it slipped back into the shadows. Armed with this knowledge I devised what I call a "back trail" camera. I mount a video camera on my shoulder facing behind me. I never turn it off so it captures everything going on behind me. On this day the back trail camera paid off and captured the footage of the Dogman.

I captured approximately fifteen seconds of the Dogman observing me in the thick foliage. It was standing upright with its head and partial left shoulder exposed. From measurements taken after the encounter the Dogman was approximately six feet tall.

The Dogman remained completely still except for one very ominous movement. I am standing still most of the fifteen seconds that I am capturing the footage but then I take a step forward. When I step forward the Dogman raises its right ear erect above its head. The motion reminded me of a dog when it hears something curious and raises or perks its ears up to listen.

Another notable physical attribute concerning the Dogman is the left ear or the lack of a left ear. The Dogman appears to have no left ear. That side of the head is completely smooth. This will be important in establishing that this subject was the same Dogman that would sneak up directly behind me less than ten minutes later in a nearby location.

I spend approximately five more minutes in the feeding station area checking the thread and looking for signs of activity.

Once I finished my observations of the area, I returned to the main trail and began walking toward the end of the point and the small island. I wanted to investigate this area because just eight months prior I had captured footage of a Bigfoot on this island. I made my way down the trail and stopped at the water's edge where the trail ended. I am using the camera I carry on a monopod to film the far shore. Little did I realize, the Dogman, that was watching me at the feeding station, had followed me to this location and was lurking only feet away in the thick foliage behind me!

First Contact Still Capture

Chapter 3 – The Close Encounter

I am now located on the shore of the lake using my monopod mounted video camera to search the small island approximately sixty feet off the main land. The foliage on both sides of the trail is extremely heavy. I actually have over hanging limbs touching the top of my head. I am in deep concentration slowly filming the adjacent shoreline looking for a possible Bigfoot.

Unknown to me, the Dogman that was observing me at the feeding station, has followed me to the water's edge. The creature has risen up only four feet behind me in the midst of a small Cedar tree. The Dogman is on the right side of the trail and my back trail camera is mounted on my left shoulder. I do not capture any footage of the creature while I am facing forward. When I decide I am done filming the island I start to turn to my left. I turn about forty-five degrees then stop for approximately six seconds. During these six seconds the Dogman is being captured on my back trail camera.

The Dogman "nervously" rocks back and forth attempting to anticipate my movement. After the six second pause I turn my shoulders further to my left and the Dogman ducks down into the heavy foliage but does not retreat. I pause again for approximately nine seconds then complete my turn. During the second nine second pause the Dogman's dark form is visible through the heavy foliage.

Once I complete my turn I get the strange feeling I am being watched. I pause momentarily and look in the exact area where the Dogman has just ducked down. I take my monopod mounted camera and film this area for approximately ten seconds. I do not see anything and after the short pause I began walking away from the area. When I review the monopod camera footage, a faint dark shape is still visible in the dense foliage. I think I was fortunate not to see the Dogman that day!

The rest of the outing went without incident. The following day I was reviewing the back trail camera footage in the comfort of my home. I remember seeing the strangely shaped creature rock back and forth as I turned my shoulders and saying to myself "what the heck was that!" I replayed the video over again this time stepping through the footage slowly. I could not believe my eyes. What was this strange thing and how did it get this close to me without making any noise? Is this a weird looking Bigfoot? I did not know that the Dogman even existed at this time.

I then loaded the footage into my video editor. I cropped around the subject and enlarged it two hundred percent. Then I adjusted the contrast and the brightness and when I played the enhanced footage back in slow motion I was horrified! I actually felt physically ill. I remember gasping and groaning out loud as I watched this "other worldly" creature moving behind me and thinking, "This thing could have killed me! It was only four of five feet behind me!"

I called to my wife to come look at the footage. When she entered the room she immediately asked me what was wrong. She said I looked extremely upset. I was almost speechless and told her "just watch, just watch this and tell me what you see." I watched as the color left her face and she gasped openly, "What in God's name is that thing?" she asked, "Where is this, where did this come from?" I told her I took the video at the public research location the day before. She then remarked, "Never go there alone and always take your gun that is a monster! No maybe a Werewolf or something evil!" I definitely agreed with her concerning taking on a research partner and carrying a firearm.

It took me several weeks to process what I had captured on video. I was genuinely afraid to go back into the woods. The more I researched this creature the more I realized how fortunate I was to have come home from the woods that day. I spent the next month investigating the Dogman. I reached out to Linda Godfrey who is the modern expert on the Dogman creature. She was very helpful and was intrigued by the video.

She assured me she had no knowledge of anyone being harmed by a Dogman. I wish I could say this was reassuring but having the footage and being the one that was so close to the creature that statement gave me little comfort.

The Dogman Still Captures

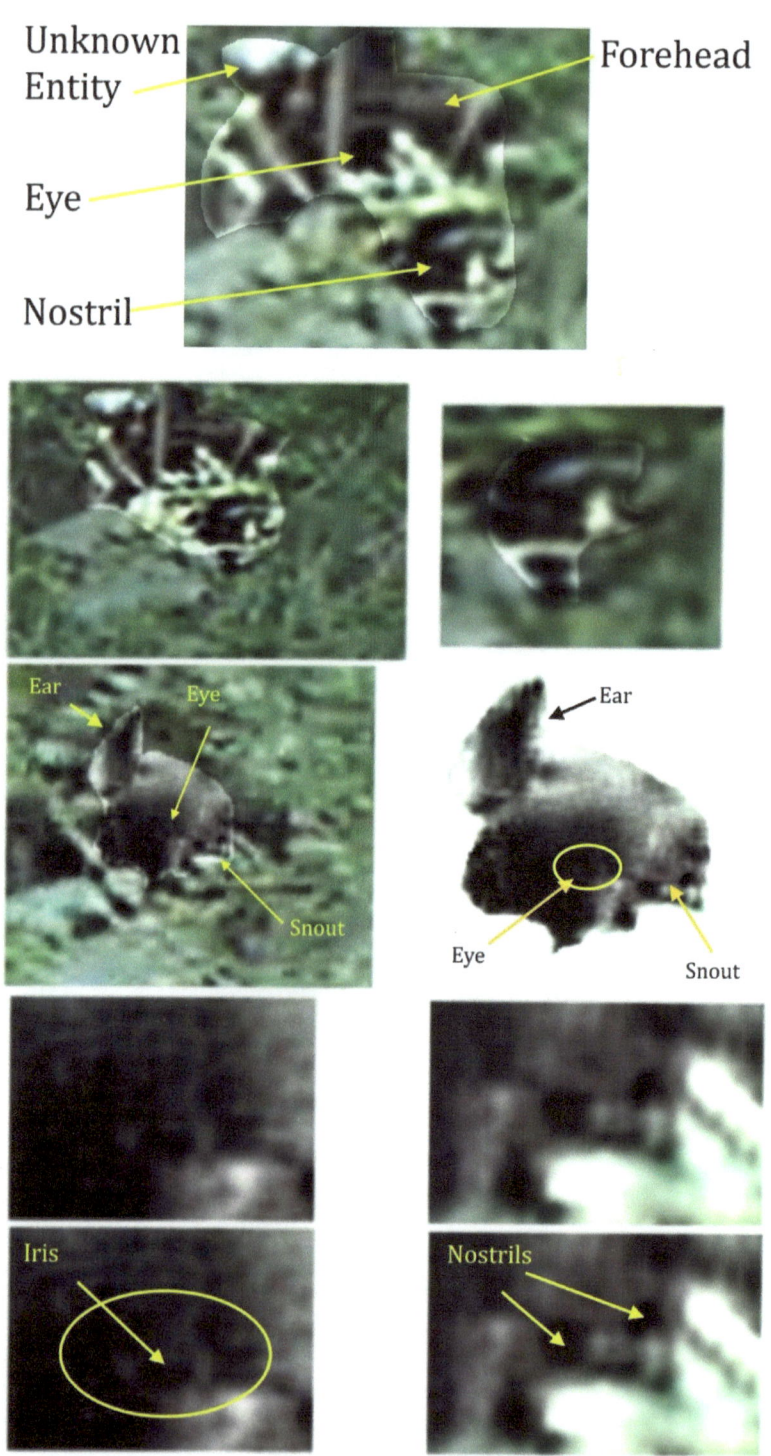

Chapter 4 - The "Devil" Is In the Details

In the weeks and months that followed I begin to break down this video in detail. The entire video clip is approximately five seconds long and at thirty frames a second I recorded one hundred and fifty frames of the Dogman creature. Not all the frames are of good quality due to the autofocus, my movement, and the creature's movement. There are however, many very clear frames.

The interesting fact about this video is how well the creature uses the natural foliage to hide its face. The creature pushes its nose through the foliage so that two limbs from the cedar tree are covering a majority of the eyes and snout. Like the Bigfoot, this creature realizes the key to recognition is the eyes. Hide the eyes, then facial recognition is extremely difficult. Though both eyes are concealed, it is obvious the creature can see through the foliage with the right eye. I also notice, at least half the nose is exposed along with the intact right ear and the top of the head. Similar to what I have noted in my Bigfoot research, the Dogman has the sensory organs exposed in order to see, hear, and smell me but also has enough of its face concealed to avoid recognition.

Details: Head Movement

In the first thirty five frames the Dogman's head is back and the nose is up in the air. I am moving my shoulders to the left during this part of the video which distorts the image but a frame by frame analysis revealed the details of the nostril openings and the right eye. The Dogman lowers its head and then pushes its snout through the vegetation. Two crossing cedar tree branches come to rest on the top of the snout. Only the end of the snout, right side of the face, and the top of the head are now exposed. The right ear is also visible. I stop my movement and the auto focus adjusts giving me the best frames of the short video.

Details: Eye Visible

After the Dogman pushes its snout through the foliage the head remains relatively still. I move my shoulders slightly and when I do this the right eye of the Dogman catches the sunlight. The iris of the eye appears to be black and "beady" in appearance. The sclera or "white of the eye" is not visible only the iris.

Details: Snout movement/Breathing

When the head is level the right end of the snout or nose is clear and visible. During approximately fifteen frames the snout can be observed opening and closing in a natural breathing motion.

Details: Photographs

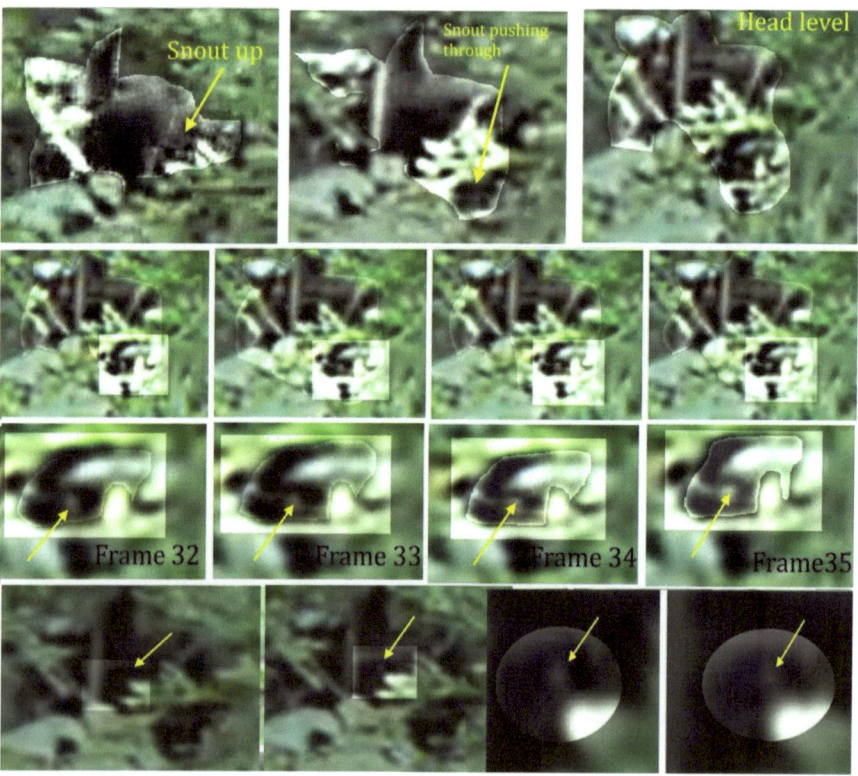

Details: The Unknown Entity

Perhaps even stranger than capturing a Dogman on video is the strange creature clinging to the side of the Dogman's head. This creature has hair or a covering on the head that is silver in appearance. The skin is a flesh tone and similar in appearance to a caucasian human. The nose is human in appearance and flat on the face. There is no snout and the nose and mouth do not protrude. The mouth also looks human. The entity resembles a human infant in the face. The head with the "bulbous" silver hair or cover gives this creature an "out of this world" appearance.

What is this unknown entity? Some have suggested it is an infant of the species clinging to the parents head and neck. Others suggest it could be an extraterrestrial biological entity. I do not know what it is. I only know it is extremely strange and that it is there.

During the encounter this unknown entity was extremely active. It moved in reaction to the Dogman's movements. It also was moving its mouth and appeared to be vocalizing to the Dogman during many frames of the clip. The video camera did not pick up any audible sounds that I can attribute to either creature but the mouth was moving in a way that suggested the unknown entity was speaking to the Dogman.

The body of this creature is small and appeared to be black in color which I found odd. I enhanced and enlarged many frames looking for any part of the body. I was looking for an arm, leg, back, or foot anything to give me an idea what this creature could be. In a limited number of frames I could see the outline of the body against the head of the Dogman. The back of the creature is visible through the foliage and at times I could see a faint glimpse of what appeared to be a small flesh colored hand grasping the side of the Dogman's head.

The unknown entity will remain one of the biggest mysteries of this video. It has been and will be the topic of much discussion and debate.

The Unknown Entity: Photographs

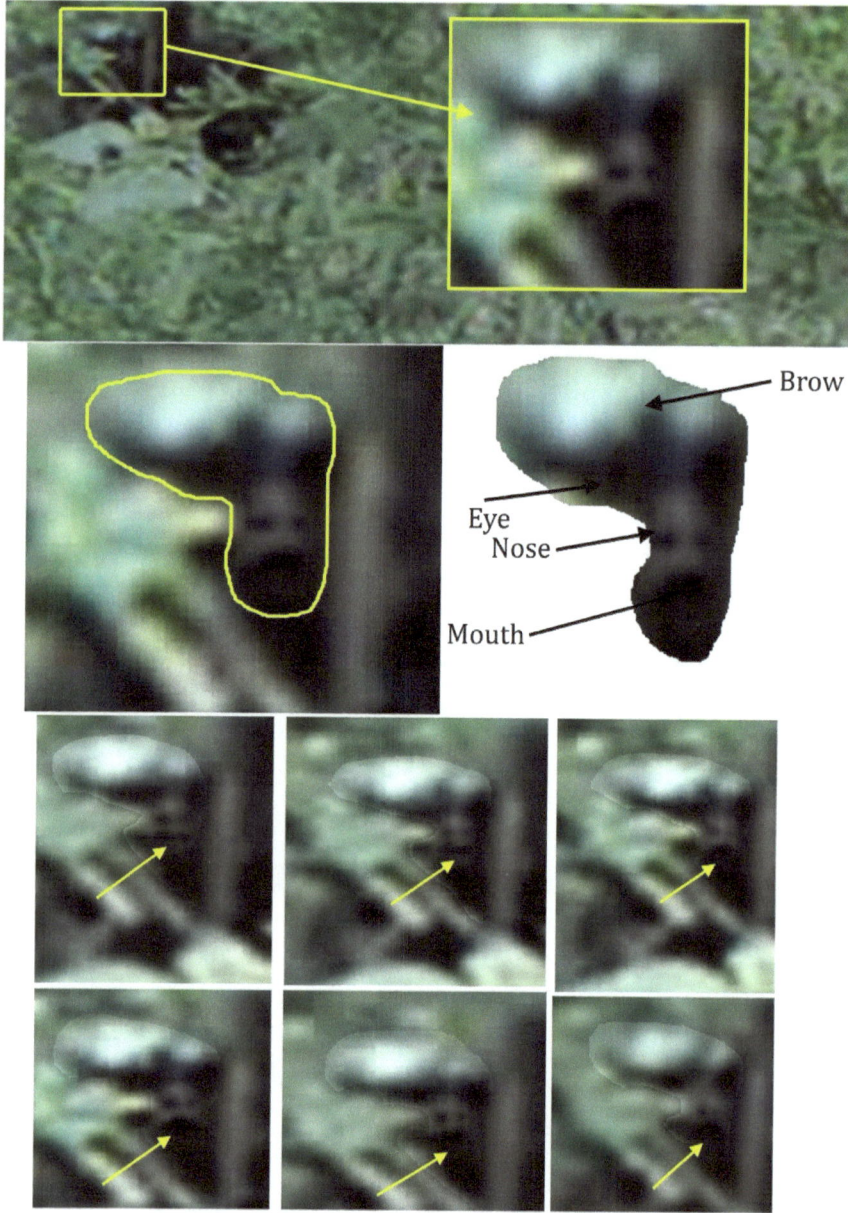

The Dogman and Unknown Entity: Sketches

Chapter 5 – Looking the Dogman in the Eye

A couple of months passed and I slowly came to grips with what I had captured on video. The reality that a creature called the Dogman actually existed sank into my brain. It changed my view of the wilderness forever. The wilderness is no longer a place of wonder and solitude. It is now a dark place where monsters lurk.

I became more cautious and began to always carry a firearm. I also noticed that the Bigfoot activity around the feeding station began to dwindle. The food I was leaving each week was not being taken. The feeling of the area changed and the shelter area began to fall into disrepair.

The rock movement started to change. I had started leaving a smiley face pattern of rocks for the Bigfoot. In the beginning of the research project the Bigfoot would push 3 rocks together and leave one separate. The smallest rock was always the one separated from the group. I interpreted that to represent "there are three of us and one of you". After the Dogman encounter the pattern changed. All the rocks were pushed to one side except for one large rock. I interpreted this to represent the Bigfoot and I are now together and the one large rock was the Dogman.

During this time I was gathering Bigfoot hair samples for the Ketchum DNA Study. I had talked with David Paulides, Director of North American Bigfoot Search, about the Dogman and we agreed it would be beneficial if I could collect hair samples of this creature. We thought that DNA from a Dogman could be as ground breaking as Bigfoot DNA.

On May 22nd, 2011 I was back in this area, firearm at the ready, as I was putting up some hair traps and setting out bacon in a jar. The bacon in a jar was an attempt to get fingerprints. I had the lid on tight but had cut holes in the lid so the smell of fresh bacon was heavy in the air.

I had the feeling I was being watched and it was not a good feeling, I felt threatened! I see something dark black about 30 feet in front of me so I take my video camera and zoom in on this black object. My heart starts pounding and I draw my weapon and chamber a round! The black object is a Dogman! It is looking at me from around a tree. It is in heavy vegetation. I am looking at it through my viewfinder on the camera, zooming in and out trying to get it in focus. Then its ears move, similar to when a dog hears a sound and begins twisting its ears. I look up over the top of the camera and make direct eye contact with this thing. I get a sick bad feeling! The eyes were strange. It was not like making eye contact with another human being. Normally when you make eye contact there is a non-verbal communication between you and the other person. There is expression, emotion, and acknowledgement. In stark contrast, the Dogman's glance was cold, black, and soulless.

I remove my side arm from the holster and chamber a round. I make sure the action makes as much noise as possible so the creature would know I was armed. When the chamber slammed back into place the Dogman immediately swiveled both ears in my direction turned its head and looked directly at me. I looked back down at the camera trying to get a better shot of the Dogman when my brain finally kicks in and I literally say to myself, "What the heck are you doing!! Get out of here now, stupid!"

I slowly begin to back out, running attack scenarios through my head. "If he charges on all fours stay calm aim for the head and shoulders, stay calm, squeeze off the shots deliberately, if he is on two legs center mass." I was convinced I was going to be attacked! To my surprise, I was able to back out of the area without incident.

My wife had dropped me off at the research area; therefore, I had no vehicle. I was walking down the trail when I called her to come and get me immediately, unfortunately, she did not answer. I wanted out of the area and wanted to be far away from this creature.

I felt like I was being followed. I continued to call over and over with no answer. So once I reached the parking area I began to walk down the access road. When my wife finally arrived, she found me already on the road out of the area. I was walking fast, gun still drawn, "white as a sheet" as she put it.

I threw my backpack into the back of the jeep and jumped in gun still drawn. "Get the heck out of here now, it may still be close." My wife looked at me puzzled and asked, "What the heck happened, what is going on!?" I replied, "Just leave NOW! I will tell you once we put some distance between us and this place!"

My wife could tell I was serious so she made a quick U-turn and we sped off quickly. We pulled into a roadside market a few minutes later and I told her what had happened. I then watched the footage on the video camera. I was both horrified and relieved that I was able to capture video of this Dogman. I showed my wife and she was shocked. She did not know what to say. We said nothing to each other the rest of the trip home.

It took a few days for me to come to grips with what had happen to me. The encounter shook me to the core. It was one thing to video a Dogman behind me but to see one and look it in the eye was mind blowing!

I knew I had to go back. I had to face my fear. I was not able to sleep and was having nightmares. The only way for me to settle the issue with the Dogman was to go back and face it down again. I called a friend who was a Bigfoot researcher and had experience with the Dogman. He was not afraid and agreed to go along.

When we arrived we made our way to the sighting area. Once in the area we looked for the tree the Dogman was hanging on. What we found was frightening. The tree had large claw marks on the sides and areas of damaged bark. You could easily see where the front claws hung in the side of the tree and where the feet were placed. I documented the findings and we left the area. I was hoping this would be my last encounter with the Dogman.

Eye Contact: Still Captures

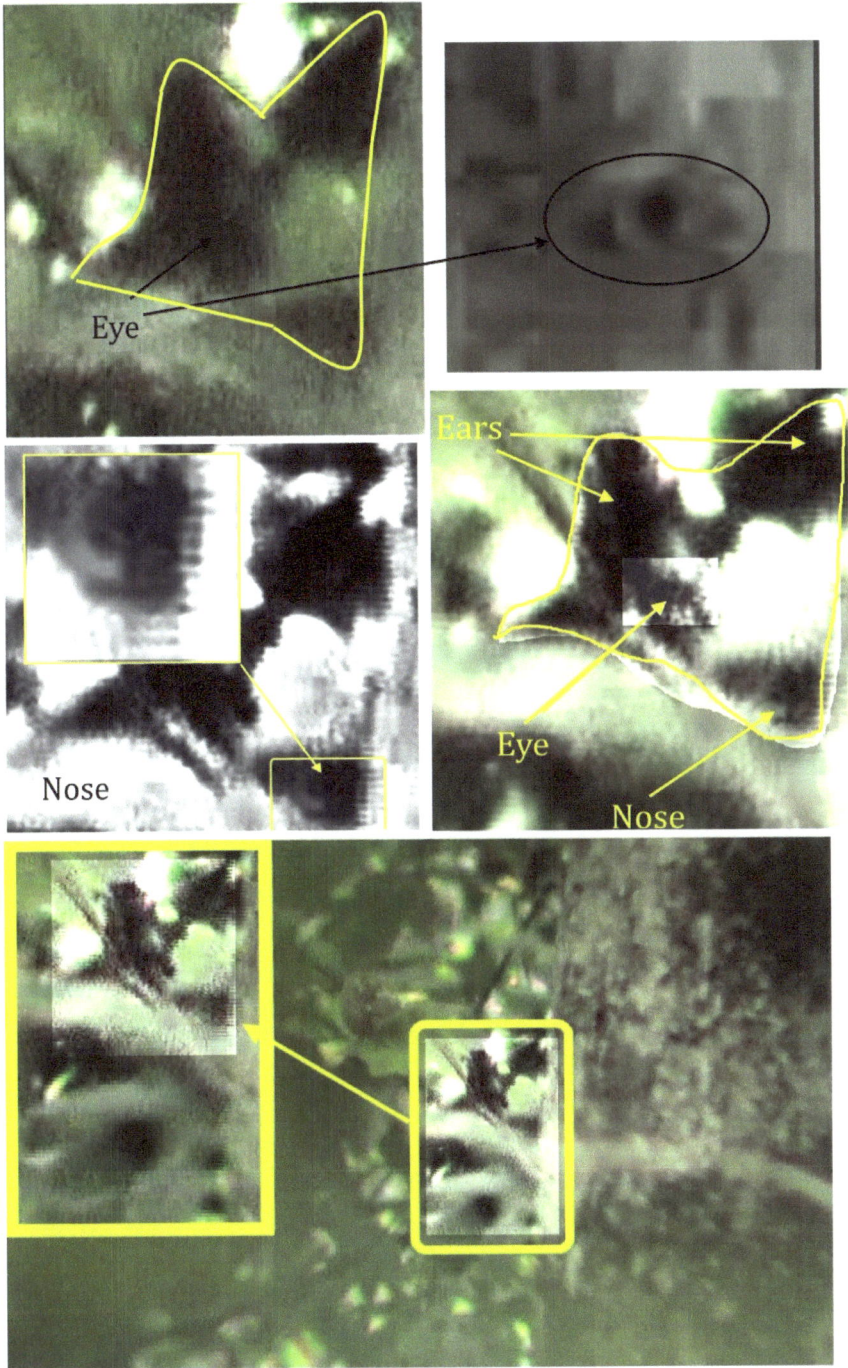

Chapter 6 – Lurking in the Shadows

The summer went by and I had no more encounters with the Dogman. I had to move the feeding station from the location of the Dogman encounters. The Bigfoot completely abandoned the area and I could find no sign of activity in that area. I found a location approximately a quarter mile away in an isolated clearing. I started leaving apples and spending time in the area. It only took a short time for the Bigfoot to discover the new feeding station. They started taking the apples and following me into this new area.

In October of 2011 I had completed my day at the public land research area. I was tired and ready to go home. I was walking quickly down a narrow side trail with my back trail camera on my shoulder filming behind me. I did not know it at the time but in the heavy foliage on the left side of the trail a Dogman was hiding. I passed within four or five feet of the creature. It only moved its mouth and blinked its eyes.

The encounter was brief but reviewing the video still gives me cold chills. This is my third encounter with the Dogman and the second time I was completely unaware of its presence.

This Dogman was all black with a short snout. The ears appeared to be short but they are difficult to see to the thick foliage. Parts of the upper and lower body are visible through the foliage. There is little detail such as arms, legs, claws, or feet. The right eye is visible and blinks during the video. The mouth is also recognizable and the Dogman opens and closes it during the footage. The Dogman also moves its entire head forward then back slightly.

The footage lasts less than two seconds and I only capture twelve clear frames.

Lurking Dogman: Still Captures

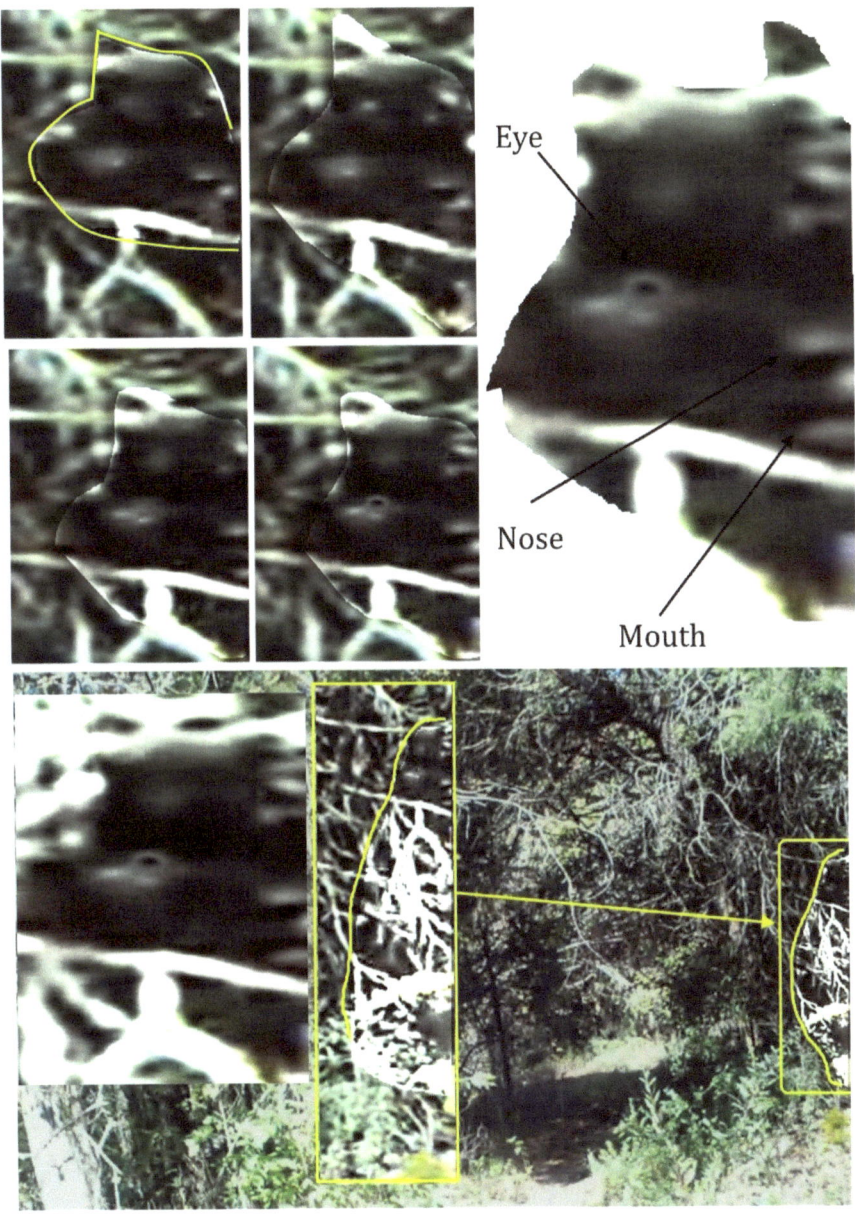

Eye

Nose

Mouth

Chapter 7 – Footprints and Glimpses

This would not be the last time I would capture video of the Dogman using the back trail camera. I thought the Dogman's home range was centered near the original feeding station. I did not think the Dogman was coming into the area where I had established the new feeding station. I had asked several "experts" on the Dogman and it was a universal opinion that Bigfoot and Dogman do not get along well. They may share the same areas but in those areas they do not comingle. Each carves out a territory and they leave each other alone. I found it interesting to note that the "experts" also agreed that the Bigfoot would leave an area and just give it over to the Dogman. The Dogman appears to be the nomadic species moving through areas and only stays for a short season. The Bigfoot tends to establish a general territory and stays in this area. The Bigfoot moves around this territory with the change of seasons but they do not migrate long distances under normal circumstances.

I found it interesting that the next time I would capture footage of the Dogman it would be close to the new feeding station. This area is active with Bigfoot activity. The Bigfoot were taking food gifts, leaving footprints, and making vocalizations in this new area. Conventional wisdom would dictate that the Dogman would either stay out of this area or the Bigfoot would move on. In this case, the Bigfoot are tolerating the incursion of the Dogman into this new area.

On March 24th, 2012 I was working my way toward the feeding station through heavy foliage. I was moving at a steady pace and was approximately fifty feet from the feeding station when my back trail camera captured the eerie image of a Dogman watching me as I walked away. This Dogman had a long slender snout, a "dog-like" looking nose, and black "beady" eyes. The appearance was similar to the Dogman I encountered eye to eye on May 22nd, 2011.

I did not sense or know that the Dogman was behind me. It was a complete surprise when I reviewed the video.

The final time I captured a Dogman on video was in April of 2012. I had started down a trail in the Great Smokey Mountains National Park with my oldest son. We stopped to look at a fallen tree on the side of the trail. While talking about the tree I captured a few frames of a Dogman watching us on our back trail camera. The creature was behind us approximately one hundred feet. It was peering over a large rock in heavy foliage. About three quarters of the face is visible but when I inverted the photographs for better detail I was amazed! The creature looked similar to a large German Shepherd with a slightly shorter snout. The ears were shorter than you would expect for a canine.

This was a sobering encounter because we were approximately three hundred feet from the parking lot. This is a major trail that is frequented by families with children. I routinely see women walking this trail alone. It concerns me this creature was this close to a high traffic trail.

Dogman: Footprints

I found two possible Dogman footprints at the public land research area. I found one on the outside of a mud hole on the point of land where I had two encounters. Approximately one year later I found a huge four toed elongated print.

The first print was four inches wide and eleven inches long. The second print was four inches wide and six inches long.

Claw marks could be seen in the ground in the larger print but I could not find any in the second smaller print.

The public land Dogman in the upper photograph and National Park Dogman in the lower photographs

Dogman Footprints

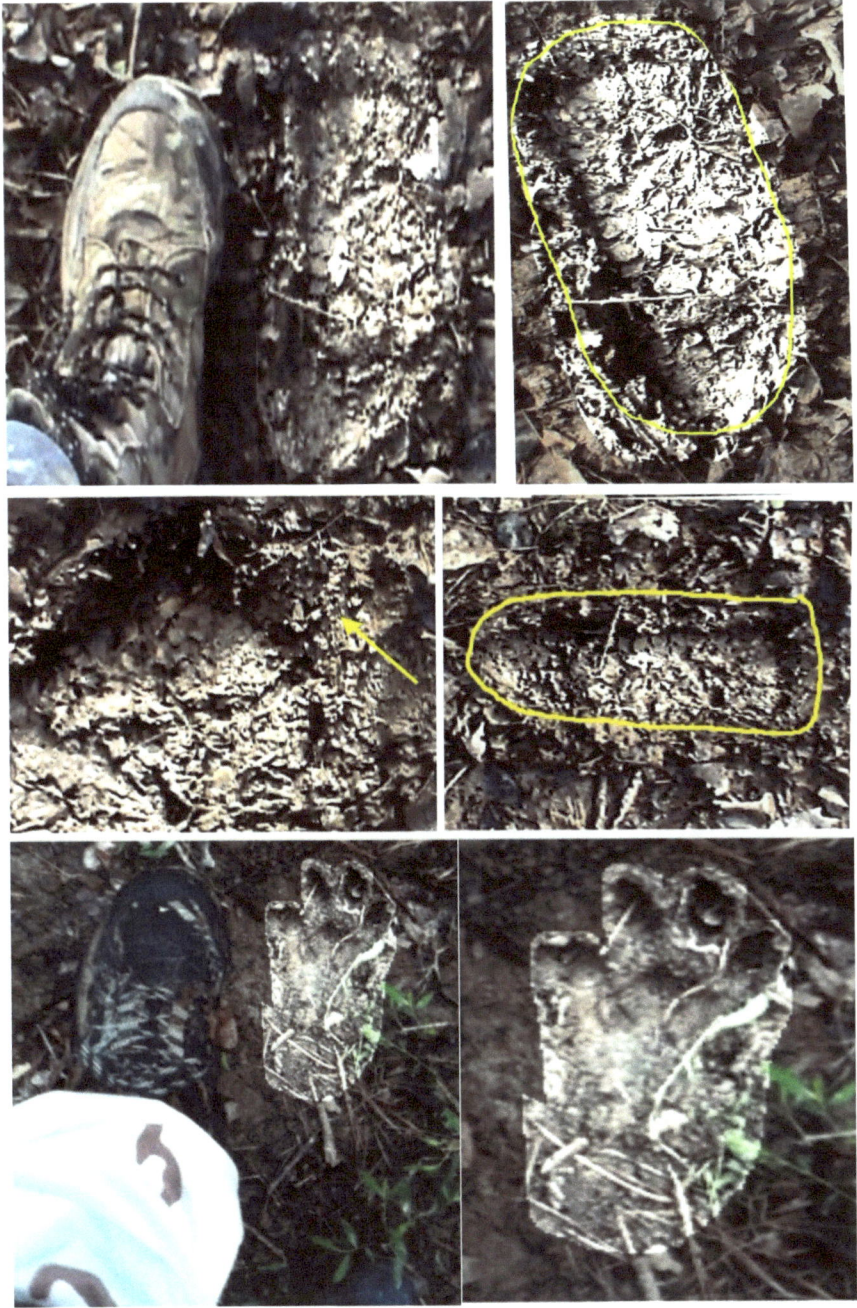

Chapter 8 – Final Thoughts

I hope this book has opened your eyes to what is actually living in the woods and wilderness area of North America. I had a hard time wrapping my mind around what I had experienced. This was not a hallucination or misidentification. I have high definition video of this creature. To add to the mystery the Dogman had this "other-worldly" Entity on its shoulder. Then only a few weeks later I have an eye witness encounter. I see it move its ears and head. I see the icy cold stare as it looks directly at me. I get the feeling I am the hunted. I am convinced I am fortunate to be alive to tell the story and show the video. This realization was a shock to my belief system. I had to re-evaluation the world and what was in it.

I know what you're thinking, "You're a Bigfoot researcher, how can you say the Dogman made you change your world view." It may sound strange but the Bigfoot is a part of the American lexicon. My generation has grown up with Bigfoot saving the world with Lee Majors on the TV show "The Million Dollar Man". The idea of a large hairy human in the wilderness was romanticized and trying to find them, for the most part, is a legitimate quest.

The Dogman on the other hand is a monster, the subject of legend, the basis for the Werewolf legend. The Bigfoot looks human, the Dogman looks like a wild beast, a predator, a "man-eater." When I captured it on video and then later saw the Dogman with my own eyes it took time to process. To be honest nothing would shock me now. I have heard rumors of other cryptids, Lizard-Man, Goat-Man, and Moth-Man.

I think now if I encounter one of these entities I will not be in shock or paralyzed by fear. I would, hopefully, be able to react to both defend myself, if necessary, and document the encounter. Encountering Dogman, as strange as this may sound, has made this possible.

I want to encourage you to question what "mainstream" science tells us about the natural world. I think a good dose of skepticism is a healthy thing. The internet is a powerful tool and I hope you will use it to do your own research. Information is no longer controlled by only a few outlets. You can now do your own research and find uncensored information. Research the alternate views and draw your own conclusions.

Videos

I have produced a YouTube video with footage of the Dogman. The video can be viewed at the following link:
https://www.youtube.com/edit?video_id=1QEOC-4lu8A&ns=1

I have also produced supporting videos with more in depth analysis:
The Dogman – Raw Footage
http://www.youtube.com/watch?v=CfUAnIrRBKM

The Dogman – The Devil's in the Details
http://www.youtube.com/watch?v=FroYFDhhoCw

The Dogman – The "Entity"
http://www.youtube.com/watch?v=hknPC5Rca40

I have also blogged extensively on my encounters. My blog address is:
http://www.bf-field-journal.blogspot.com/

Reference Material

Linda Godfrey
http://lindagodfrey.com/

http://www.beastofbrayroad.com/

www.ingramcontent.com/pod-product-compliance
Lightning Source LLC
Chambersburg PA
CBHW042239290526
45792CB00021B/824